CEREMONY

Poetry & Prose

BRIANNA WIEST

THOUGHT CATALOG Books

THOUGHTCATALOG.COM
NEW YORK · LOS ANGELES

THOUGHT
CATALOG
Books

Copyright © 2021 Brianna Wiest.
All rights reserved.

Published by Thought Catalog Books,
an imprint of the digital magazine
Thought Catalog, which is owned and
operated by The Thought & Expression
Company LLC, an independent media
organization based in Brooklyn, New
York and Los Angeles, California.

This book was produced by Chris
Lavergne and Noelle Beams. Cover art
and typesetting by KJ Parish. Special
thanks to Isidoros Karamitopoulos for
circulation management.

thoughtcatalog.com
shopcatalog.com

Made in the USA
ISBN 978-1-949759-33-4

For Stephen — who will always be everything to me.

The light does not choose who to shine upon
it beams, it radiates, it spreads to every open space
all of the grass on the entire earth
does not have to compete
for the rays of sun that nourish it
there is enough for every blade
all the billions of them
and that is the lesson

The grasses don't stop growing
because they fear wildfires
or the stomping of wild cows
if it comes, it comes
you can't hold your breath wondering,
what if I fall from the edge?
what if you never see the view?
which question do you want to haunt you?

Fearlessness is the willingness
to love the things that you will eventually lose
which are all things,
even the blood and bones of you

The healing is not the destruction. It is not the day you know it is finally time to uproot your life. It is not the moment you tell someone they are no longer welcome, it is not the hours you spend decluttering, it is not the minute you walk away. The healing is how you gradually allow your soul to drip into your days again. It is how you show up more fully now that the debris is cleared, and the roads are unblocked, and your life is once again renewed and refreshed and freed. It was never about whether or not you had the courage to light fire to what was, it was whether or not you were willing to plant a seed in its place, and to grow what was always meant to be.

Other people are not
here to love us
in the exact way we
think they should
they are here to set up
a healing ceremony
at which we learn how
to love ourselves

Just because it wasn't forever
doesn't mean it wasn't
destined for you

The real love story was always you and you. It was how you walked alone and learned what you needed to carry. It was how you began to see through your own eyes, and not someone else's. It was how you began to dig joy out from beneath your cynicism, how you slowly built your desires into form. It was how you learned what you like and don't, and what you came here to be. The real love story was always how you opened your heart to yourself.

When you are in a rebirth, you don't know you're being reborn. All you know is that something inside of you is dying. That is the only thing that feels real.

It feels so real that it makes you believe it will go on forever. It feels so real that you begin to distrust everything you thought you knew before. It wraps itself around your mind until it's the only thing you can see. All there is to do is accept it, and wait while it gradually eases. Despite your disbelief, will always ease.

When you are in a rebirth, you aren't reborn just once. It comes in waves and layers. You let go and then you let go a little bit more. Without even realizing what is happening, the new pieces of your life begin to emerge. You stumble upon the things that feel so right, you almost wonder if they're too good to be true. You don't let yourself settle into any certainty. Slowly, you begin to see what must go, how the world around you must now change to match the changed one within you.

Eventually, you find yourself standing firmly within all you feared would never come. One day, you wake up on the other side. It is at this moment that you must remember the truth you forgot at the beginning: we didn't come here to suffer, we came here to grow. When we resist the elements of growth—when we are too attached to what must pass—we end up stuck and longing. The truth is that life will change, and we will eventually harvest every seed of effort and love and truth we ever planted. *When we ask to greet a new horizon, we have to learn to embrace the journey that will get us there.*

We are always a thought away
from a healing notion
that can cast a ripple of waves
across the entire universe

The present moment is the entryway
to all that you've ever wanted

*stillness is the entryway
to the present moment*

The universe is not making you wait
for what will be yours
you are waiting on your own readiness,
and it's okay if that takes time

You don't fall in love with yourself by convincing yourself you are nothing but goodness. You don't heal the holes in your heart by telling yourself they don't exist. You don't just begin believing in your own perfection one day. You fall in love with yourself when you fall in love with the smallest details of your life. You fall in love with yourself when you start to take care of yourself. *You fall in love with yourself when you stop thinking of self-love as an infatuation, but as a homecoming.* You fall in love with yourself when the child inside looks at the adult you are now and sees the ease of their own approval.

All things exist in perfect duality
with equal and opposite force
your most daring dreams
will strike fear in your heart
in ways you've never known
sometimes, this is not a sign to turn away
but to keep walking

The unknown is also the
realm of infinite potential

What if, just for today, you did not worry
just for tonight, you set aside your cares
tomorrow you can worry
you can worry about everything on your list
you can worry for every hour you're awake
but what if just for today
you decided you'd worry tomorrow
and then you woke up tomorrow
and did the same thing

We don't let go when we have found every answer. We don't let go when we finally arrive at every reason, every purpose. We don't let go when we understand every bit of meaning behind everything we've ever been through. We let go when we realize we do not need to know everything in order to loosen our grip on life. We let go when we realize that not everything has to make perfect sense in order to be perfectly right for us. We let go when we realize that we cannot overthink our way into releasing—we can simply open our hands and allow the rest to fall as it may.

"What is this feeling here to teach me?"
—*Becoming*

There are moments so perfect
I try to suspend them in the air
that is when I know I am dying
I know I am a wave breaking and destined to recede
maybe that's why I'm so in love with it all
I know that anywhere I arrive
is a peak in time before returning

Hold a steady image of the future in your mind. Hold it far beyond what's reasonable for a daydream. Hold it so long that it begins to feel real. Hold it until you think it just might be. Hold it until your mind begins to weave together possibility, drawing pathways from that mountaintop to where you stand today. Hold a steady image of the future in your mind, because it is only after we identify the destination that the journey can truly begin.

Letting go is not the end,
it is the beginning

What if there is a path for you that is greater than what you can envision? What if there is a life for you that is more than you would even know to ask for? What if you are inherently and unknowingly limited by your old perspectives, your outdated ideas of what is possible? What if all the discomfort within your being is simply trying to redirect you to a place beyond anything you've considered before? What if there is more than you know? What if there are things out there so good, you don't even know you're waiting for them?

The past that you believe is currently holding you back is nothing but a memory. It's an image that lives in your mind and in your mind alone. The past is not a painting in a museum. It is not a portrait that we can gaze at and identify each brushstroke and contour. It is a semblance of emotion, a series of recollection, most of which become increasingly more distorted over time.

Do you ever wonder why the things that seem to drum up your heartbeat and sink your stomach until you're caving in on yourself are one dimensional ideas of what might have happened, or how someone may have seen it? Out of your entire life, why is it that that some experiences carry so much weight over all the others? Why is it that you've distilled a memory down to its most haunting form? Is this the full truth of your story?

I want you to feel into your body. Feel the tension and constriction in your bones. Feel the weight of what you have been carrying for all of these years. Feel your feet and your legs and your hips and your neck. Feel the contractions, how your cells are constructing your body as the first line of a defense in a battle that is long, long over.

As you feel this more and more deeply, I want you to tell yourself something over and over again.

The past is gone, all that exists is this moment.

The past is gone and when we try to resurrect pieces of it without its full context, we hurt ourselves for no reason. There is no wisdom to be gained this way. There is no lesson to be learned. There is nothing that is added to our current lives nor our future ones, there is only time that is taken away. The past is gone and when we try to let our most impulsive thoughts tell us what it was or what it meant, we rob ourselves of the experience that was our own life.

Every step, every chance, every person, every encounter, and even everything you think you did wrong was building the person that you would one day become. Before you start thinking that good people can only be a collection of positive experiences, please remember that you often must first realize what is wrong before you will know what is right. You must know what love isn't to know what love is. You must be who you aren't to discover who you are.

Instead of belittling the version of you that was holding themselves up in whatever way they knew how, thank them. The vision of your future rested within their minds. You are only here today because of what they did, and how they did it.

Could you imagine if they knew, that after all of that, their future selves would look back on them and sum them up by the smallest details that they couldn't even control?

You owe yourself more than this.

You owe your life more than this.

It's time to let go of the past, though of course, it's already gone. There's nothing that you have to release other than your idea that these old experiences are still with you now, because they aren't. There's nothing that you have to release other than the fact that your life is not just one thing. When we carry the past into the present, it's because the experience feels unfinished. But what we often don't realize is that the only way to complete it is to take everything we wish we could have had then and to pursue it completely right now.

The most damaging way to live is not to stay small so that the world is never given the opportunity to hurt us on occasion, but that we hurt ourselves every day insisting that we might not be able to start living now because something behind us once didn't go as we planned.

Courage is to show up and live anyway.

Change is to show up and live anyway.

Truth is to show up and live anyway.

The memories will keep coming, for a while. They don't leave because we tell them to. They slowly fade as we fill our minds with new things more captivating, more compelling, more worth our attention.

We do not let go by standing within the ruins, but by building the life that was trying to emerge all along.

You don't heal some things
you just start living in
spite of their presence
which is when they
heal themselves

Everything seems ordinary
until you have tried to grasp a galaxy
or imagine it above your own head

Could you imagine orchestrating the bloom of a rose
in sync with the seasons?
Do you know what it is
that makes the tea seep
or what connects the neurons in your mind?
Perhaps your beating heart fuels your body
but from what idea did the aorta come?

Maybe genius is when we realize
what seems so simple on the surface
is a work of the most intense and illusive mastery
if we only gaze just beneath

Joy is a form of rebellion

We are born through
each others' bodies
maybe we awaken through
each others' souls

Your life is your own. I want you to read that sentence until it sinks all the way down inside your gut and meets every last impulse that tells you to put your intuition on pause, to place yourself second, to squeeze and bend and break into the molds of what everyone else wants you to be. *Your life is your own.* I want it to pass through your head so many times it slowly clears out the debris of your fear. I want you to meditate on it until you realize that you are not too strange, you just have the courage to be your true self; you are not too different, you just have the courage to follow your own heart; you are not unworthy, you are just honest about the very natural, human experience of feeling unworthiness. Every person alive wishes to embody these very same forms of freedom. They are not judging you, they are expressing the parts of themselves they've judged into silence. *Your life is your own,* and it always will be. You must find the courage to claim it, or it will pass by you untouched—a glimmering, lost potential of all that could have been.

The truth is that if we want to make a big leap forward, we are often first asked to first take a small step back. If we carried on undisrupted, there would be no impetus for change. There would be nothing to make us stop and second guess where we're headed. There would be nothing to direct us off the familiar path. There would be nothing to spark the unraveling of what we've been, and the becoming of what we will be. There would be nothing to initiate progress. If somewhere deep within you, you are asking life to rise up to the next level, you will often first be asked to sink down into what's holding you within this one.

You will not be the same
person a year from now
you must decide which
way you will grow

I wonder if the trees ever fear the rain won't come
I wonder if they would count each cloud
recall all the times it rained prior
or trace each root as it gradually dried
wondering and worrying
will the storm come again and heal me?

Of course, the trees are far more advanced than us
they have no such concern
the river of life never stops flowing
and it flows through us
and into all we need

When I was young I was so angry
wanting everyone to be just like me
now I just tilt my head back and laugh
as though the cypress demands
the cedar spread its thistle wider
not realizing they are all evergreen

You change your life at the
same pace you change the story
you tell yourself about it

In the end, you must learn to take care of yourself first. You must throw away the idea that doing so is selfish; you were taught such things by people who had to justify their own lack of self-actualization. You will never be as far away from helping someone else than when you are in need of help, and you will never find hurting another as easily excusable as when you yourself are hurt. If there is nothing else in this world that you can even find a semblance of control over, begin a journey to your own inner peace. It will do more than you know.

All things arrive in their own timing
all questions will be answered
slowly, you will let go
even if it feels impossible right now
slowly, you will move on
whether you know how to or not
all things arrive in their own timing
and that includes you

I am a temple unto myself
my body is my home
I am my own safe space
within me is the access point
to all that is and will ever be
I greet it not to amend it
but to return home for a moment
to distill myself to my source
to ease the line between
where my skin ends
and the world begins

Even if you feel you are falling behind, even if you are not where you thought you'd be, even if nothing turned out the way you thought it would, it does not mean you are not still growing. Real growth is not always just constant forward motion, it's also staying still. Growth is learning the hard lessons. Growth is deep rest. Growth is stopping to reconsider where you're headed before you arrive there. Growth is letting yourself settle, it's letting yourself blossom, it's letting yourself see how much good is already in your life before you hunger for more.

You are more than the sum
of how others see you

If your mental health
has ever failed you
if the pieces meant to support you
were collapsing faster
than you could put them back together
if you have ever looked into the mirror
and could not recognize who was looking back
if you have ever tried to ask for help
and were met with disbelief
if you ever came closer than you ever thought
to wondering why you might remain alive
if you have ever found it
nearly impossible to rise
and face a world
that does not believe you are in pain
I have been there, with you
and there is another side

Reviewing the details one more time will not change the outcome. If there was an answer, you would have found it. If there was more to learn, you would have learned it. Not all stories end in a way we understand, but that doesn't mean that they aren't finished. Some things happen in random timing, and without a clear reason, and for a purpose that remains unknown. If you needed to know, you already would. Keep walking.

Your story is not to be written as a novel
you are a collection of the people you've become
and the people you've yet to be
a series of stories told in sequence
sometimes with rhyme
and sometimes without reason
a neverending exploration
of every corner of your potential
please don't worry
if you cannot converge your old selves
you are not meant to understand them
you are only meant to set them free

If more people found
the courage to share the
stories within their souls,
the world would be
a better place

If you could only see how
magnificently you've grown
if you could only see
how far you've come

The soul of what you are seeking is subtle. Success is subtle, beauty is subtle, purpose is subtle. Everything real is often quite subtle, which is what makes it so elusive, which is what makes it so easy to miss.

You are allowed to let go of your old dreams.

You are allowed to redesign your plan for your life. What you decided upon years ago was chosen for a person you no longer are.

You were not born to do just one job, play just one role, be just one person, stay in just one place. You are a constant evolution. You are a continual unfolding. You haven't met every part of yourself yet, you haven't unearthed every desire. There is more to you, and there is more to life—but to know this, you have to do the first and most subversive thing, which is to leap without knowing exactly where you will land. What do you want your most ordinary days to look like? That's your true dream, and you should pursue it. Chase what's right for the person you are now, knowing you are still free to choose something else for the person you will one day become.

You are allowed to change.

You are allowed to be different than you were before.

You have not failed your younger self.

You saved them.

Playing small never kept you safe
it only denied you your own love
it only denied you your own life

You are allowed to not know. You are allowed to make a life within the questions. The stories that are told so fluidly, the paths that are so clear—they are the ones already fully walked. They, too, were filled with doubt at the beginning. Don't worry about fitting every piece into the picture. Take one more step forward each day, and the rest will fall into place over time.

Do not ever allow the fear of being something imperfectly prevent you from becoming anything at all

Growth means letting go of
the person who has kept you
safe in order to become the
one who can set you free

You can have all of the doubt in the world
and still be on the right path
you can feel all the fear in the world
and still be perfectly safe
you can harbor all the of the self-hatred in the world
and still be perfectly loved
what you feel is always valid
but it isn't always real

Finding yourself is not an immediately beautiful thing. It's less meeting your soul at the mountaintop and more sorting through the debris that prevents you from seeing the path. It's less falling into peacefulness and more confronting the inner voices that stir up self-loathing. It's less revelations, and more honestly allowing the heaviest thoughts to simply pass without taking action that disrupts your day. I know it is counterintuitive, but finding yourself is one of the hardest things you will ever do—and it is also the most life-giving. There is nothing else that will bring you back home to yourself.

How do you figure out who you are?

You stay right where you are. You dig. You learn the simplest facts about yourself. You date yourself. You daydream until you discover something that makes your chest feel even the smallest spark of hope. You question your darkest thoughts. You create rituals, soul-opening routines. You begin exactly where you are, with exactly what you have, and you work until every detail is made beautiful. You let yourself feel what you feel. You begin to act in self-loving ways even, and maybe most especially, when you fear you don't deserve it. You realize that you are growing through the discomfort. You learn to let yourself be.

You don't always have to be strong, not in the way you think strength exists. Sometimes, strength is lowering your defenses and letting your lips shake. Sometimes, it is folding into yourself, letting yourself ache. Strength is not the will to override being human, but the willingness to accept it. It is painting the picture with contrast, with depth, and with soul.

You are more powerful
than you realize
there is more within you
than you know

In stillness, you receive guidance
in effortlessness, you know what's right for you
in serendipity, you find what's on your path
in acceptance, you receive everything there is

You did not come here to be perfect. You did not come here to smooth out every line and crease of your heart. You did not come here to step in perfect succession, with one milestone preceding the next, forever onward, until you arrive at death, right on time, having bothered as few people as possible. This is not what you are here for. This is not what you came to do. You were not born to rush through your becoming just to reach the other side. You were not born to be instantaneously perfected, but to piece yourself together slowly over time.

Your growth has never bowed in the wrong direction
nobody questions the curves of a river's course
you have only become more yourself
you have only become more free

Know the depth of your power
and use it with lightness
and give it to kindness
and make of it love

Your body is the first temple
and you would not let the temple go uncleaned
you would not let the temple go undecorated
your body is the only place
your becoming will occur
it is your closest mirror
your first and last companion
the vessel of all that you will ever be

Your life is not just
meant to be documented,
it's meant to be lived

If you cannot imagine what you'd pack in a single bag if that's all you could carry, then you don't know yourself very well at all.

The point is not that you might one day arrive at a place where there is no pain, because that would be a lifeless state. The point is that when pain arrives, you greet it like an old friend. You nurse it through the night. You talk with it until its roots are revealed. You allow it to give you guidance and wisdom. You allow it to humble you. You allow it to remind you that life might be hard, but love is a healing force—and there is no love as powerful as your own.

How to change your life

Read. A book you read this weekend can change your life for decades to come. If you can't read, listen. Find podcasts, speeches, essays, anything that opens your mind and makes you consider something you didn't before. Decide what is going to matter to you. Pick a few things you're going to devote your life to and let go of everything else. Study the greats, the ones who have walked the path before you. Draft a vision of your highest potential future self, and then trace the elements of their lives back to where you are right now. Embody them slowly. Notice what makes you most envious—this is what you truly want. Notice what makes you feel most regretful—this is what you need to do next. Write down three facts you'd like to be true about yourself and repeat them to yourself every day in the present tense. Be ambitious. Remember that the way you saw life lived was not how existence must be. Let yourself grieve. Get rid of the clutter, both mental and physical. Draw outside the lines. Break the chains. Remember why you came here, and what you were meant to do.

This is the day your life begins.

Though of course, it never really stopped.

Somewhere in the course of your journey you got the idea that you had to spend some period of time in a limbo, a purgatory, a prep period, a waiting room, in which you would have to earn your own joy. You got the idea that until you were good enough, you did not deserve to savor the little things, which are really the big things. You got it in your head that you were destined to spend some period of time simply sitting on the sidelines until someone invited you to play the game.

Today, that changes. Today your life begins, because you are no longer waiting until it is perfect before you begin to participate.

You are not a project. You are also not a robot. The real work of improving yourself can only be done in real time, through trial and error, by showing up and sometimes getting it wrong.

The people who never misstep are the ones who have never tried anything meaningful. What may look like a flawless record on the surface is deep and pervasive longing just beneath. But I promise you, this will not be your story, because your life begins today.

What you lose when you think that you cannot yet show up to your own life is the ability to actually live it. You lose the notion that any one moment can be the instance that changes it all. Because that's exactly how it happens. One day, you meet the love of your life. One day, you apply for the job of your dreams. One day, you're standing in the tarmak, one day, you're landing in a new country, one day, you're packing your bags, one day you get the keys, one day you get the good news. One day, you submit the manuscript. One day, a tipping point is hit and you are forever changed.

Your entire life is a series of moments, not in the past or future, but unfolding in the infinite now, all of which are giving you micro-opportunities, portals to become the person you have always wanted to be, which really means, living the life you have always wanted.

Because you have been waiting to start, you have replaced your genuine desires for life with ideas about what a perfect life might look like, as opposed to how it would feel. Work will always be work. Relationships will always be relationships. The parties will end, and nobody will know what was in your bank account or wasn't, nobody will check the tags of your clothes to see where they are from, and nobody will even remember what you wore there anyway, because of course, they were too busy worrying about themselves.

Do you want to know the truth?

There is not one more thing that you need to do in order to be good enough for your own life. There is not one more thing you need to earn, accomplish, acquire or change.

The only finish line you're rushing toward is death.

If you're under the impression that you will only ever be able to feel happy when you create the very specific experiences you envision in your mind, you are incorrect. Happiness is a practice. If we don't learn how to appreciate what we have while we have it, nothing will be enough. So what you are risking is more than just missing yet another day walking in circles around yourself, fixing things that aren't really broken, anxious about missing out on updates about other people's lives while you stare at your phone and miss your own. What you are risking is arriving to all of the places you have ever dreamed and realizing that you are no happier for being there.

Please don't let that be your story.

Please don't let your days pass you by.

Please let your life start today.

Please make today the day that changes the rest of your days to come.

The people, places and things that are destined for you are the ones that give you as much energy as they take. What's meant for us becomes a symbiotic force—when we move toward what's right, what's right moves toward us.

It is okay if you are still healing
into the person you want to be

We all assume that because we live in such a hyper-connected society, we should be less lonely than ever. Not only can we keep in touch with everyone we've ever known, but we can witness every detail of their lives unfold before us. No human beings prior to this ever experienced the world in such a way. *That's exactly the problem.* What we gain in connection, we lose in context. We are stuck bridging all of our old identities into one. It's hard to move on. It's hard to let go. We are strangers to ourselves, because in a world where everyone is watching, we are more pieces of what they would want us to be than the whole of who we really are.

If you keep reaching for dreams that are in the future, you will always be left empty in the now. Reality can never feel quite as compelling as the imagination. This doesn't mean that we can't aspire—it just means that we should aspire to the moment. It means that we should put all of our effort into making each day the very best it can be. Real change can only occur in the quiet, ordinary moments that too easily pass by.

The mountain often
hides within it the magic
we had been asking for all along

It's time to forgive yourself for the things that you did when you didn't know better, for the choices you made when you did not realize there were any other options, for the person you were when you did not yet know who to be. There is no path that is seamless in this life, no course that does not come without turns and the occasional dead end.

There is nothing to be gained by punishing yourself. There is no wisdom, no knowledge, no goodness, and no betterment that can come from this kind of mindset. You are not making up for what you didn't do well enough. You are not proving how much you've grown. You are not safeguarding yourself from ever making a mistake again.

All you are doing is proving that you have not yet fully learned what you need to know.

When we have truly moved on, we do so by understanding that we are always doing the very best with what we have.

Our younger selves were not meant to be perfect. They were simply people acting on the beliefs they had before they knew how to question them, the feelings they felt to before they knew how to manage them.

Your younger self is not the unfinished, inferior version of you. They carried you all this way. Despite all of their shortcomings, they are still the hero of your life. The vision of your future, of all that you had yet to see, was dormant within them. They are the ones who brought you here now.

The time you took was the time you needed. The person you were was the person you had to be. Forgive yourself for the person you were when you were trying to get by. This is not part of you to hide, it is part of you to honor. It is the person who got you to the other side.

You are a steady stream
of every idea you might make real
it is only a matter of what you do with them
it is only a matter of when you arrive

Each time you correct a fearful
thought, you plant a seed of healing

I hope that you find the courage to gently start over.

Sometimes, starting over is an abrupt ending. It is rising one morning and by the time the sun is setting you clearly see that you must leave. You must change where you are and who you are and what you do, because your existing life has so little of your soul within it, it's leaving you as a shell of the person you might be.

Then there's the kind of starting over where we begin to understand that all the successes we might crave—in love, and in work, and in ourselves—are really just a matter of constantly trying new things until we get it right. Because for every one thing that works, there will be a thousand that don't. You just don't hear people tell stories about those things. This is the kind of starting over that leaves you scrapping the manuscript three times, restarting the business, renovating, then tweaking, then coming up with a more aligned and supportive vision, and then reinventing, and then implementing, and then seeing what sticks. This is the kind of starting over that's all about adaptation. You know that you have a good thing, or a passion, or a truth, and all you're really trying to find is the right way to make it real within the world. Because no path is a straight line, and if we want to stay on it, we have to bend, lest we break.

Then there's the kind of starting over that's the most important of all. And that's the kind you do each day. That's the kind where the changes are so subtle, you might not even notice them at all. But these are the shifts that actually change your life. This is the way you slowly learn over time how to style that natural wave in your hair you always hated and have now decided it's time to learn to love. This is the way that you slowly learn to savor each sip of your morning coffee and to sit in silence and be grateful that life has given you another day to live it. This is the way that you begin to speak and respond to the people you love as the person you hope to be. One big motion does not make for a breakthrough; it is a tipping point, and a tipping point is a collection of small changes.

If you are not willing to start over in the smallest moments of your life, and in the gentlest and most unassuming of ways, when your flight lands in the new city, your habits will come with you. Every new blueprint you draw will have within it the same old design. Every road will lead to the same destination because you have not really changed the way you travel, and to where.

Your story is not over. You are not the sum of the people you used to be, you are not the sum of the way other people see you, and you are not the sum of what you think you are capable of right now.

I hope that you learn you do not need to wait for a huge wave of motivation, you do not need to wait until you are absolutely ready or confident or sure.

Find the simplest change you can, and then make it.

Wake up tomorrow, and do it again.

You are not what you became when you were most afraid. You are what flows through you when you are most joyful, most inspired. You are what you feel when everything feels at ease. You are what you know when that quiet, little voice inside tells you—*it's going to be ok*. You are not the person you became to cope with the life you didn't ask for. You are the person you choose to become in the life you build despite it.

Just because you can
feel every burden
does not mean that they
are all yours to carry

What if, in the moments you feel most alone, you began to realize that you are also free?

What if you could finally see that in the very times you are on your own, you are also completely unburdened from the expectations of others, able to define and rede-fine yourself, to explore life on your own terms, to finally hear the sound of your own voice? What if you've already made it? What if instead of believing your aloneness is a sign you have failed, you realize that it is also proof you have accomplished the most daring task of all?

What if, instead of believing that you must be the best to be good enough, you realized that to wake up and have something to do is a purpose and gift that should never be taken for granted? What if, instead of believing that you have failed, you began to recognize that failure is just life's way of moving you in a different direction? What if, instead of thinking that your life was meant to unfold seamlessly, you realized that the courage it takes to keep opening doors, even if they all close, is all part of the process? What if, instead of losing hope in the world and life itself, you allowed your failures to strengthen your faith, making you see that there is a path for you to walk, and a forcefield holding you to it, no matter how hard you may try to get off?

What if you realized that other people are under no ob-ligation to be who you think they should be, and the most loving thing you could do would be to set them free in your own mind? What if you realized that they didn't have to be precisely as you imagine in order for you to exchange the love you are meant to share, in order for you to be okay? What if the journey is really asking you to love flawed people, so you might be able to love your flaws the same way?

What if your body appears precisely the way it is meant to? What if you believe that there's something wrong with the way you look because you've spent an excessive amount of time fantasizing about how light and free perfection would feel? What if all you needed to do was simply look around you? To the people you know, the people you don't, the people who coexist in the world beside you? What if you truly began to realize that almost nobody exists within that fantasy, and yet so many are still deeply and completely loved, fully alive and happy, walking in their truth and thriving as all they were meant to be?

What if the life of your dreams is not one where you do all things perfectly for an audience within your own imagination, but one where you have a few things you care about deeply and passionately and spend your life with them, releasing into the nothingless all the other cares that did nothing but hold you back from your own love and life?

When we are not writing the
story of this chapter,
we give our minds no choice but to
continue reading the last one

The ones who hurt you were they themselves wounded, often far beyond anything you can comprehend. This understanding does not excuse, it simply explains. It explains that it wasn't you, it was a reflection of them. It explains that some of the ways life can be most unfair is when we are collateral damage to a storm we did not create, and yet, have been asked to weather. The ones who hurt you were they themselves wounded, and there is nothing you can do about this fact. There is only one decision, which is to ask yourself if you will stand here forever, or walk forward into your own light.

One day, you will have to reinvent yourself outside of the shadow of what everyone else has asked you to be. You will have to ask yourself who you are if you had no obligation to anyone else. You will have to explore who you would become if you knew you were completely free, if you knew you would not be judged, if you knew that all the things you ever desired were simply on the other side of you stepping into who you already are— taking the essence of your soul and turning it into form.

The ones who cannot
meet your soul where it is are
not the ones who will walk you
to where you are meant to be

When you are young, you are taught to look for the most striking forms of love, the ones that knock you off your feet and take your breath away. But when you get back up, you slowly come to find that the love that is truly worthwhile is not the one that throws you off your path, but holds your hand and walks with you on it. This is the love that grows with time, not fades. This is the love that goes just a bit deeper each time the tide goes out, and introduces you to parts of yourself you didn't know existed. This is the love you are waiting for. Not the sparks on the surface, but the fire that's slowly kindled just beneath.

Niceness soothes, but kindness heals. Niceness often tells us what we want to hear, while kindness tells us what we need to know. I know it is easier to walk through your life in niceness, to be as the world would wish, to speak as someone else would have you. I know that you spent your life being conditioned into niceness, but the kindest thing you could possibly do is to speak truth, as boldly as you can, and firstly, to yourself.

If you would like to change your life, you must first change the way you think about your life. Thoughts are not just thoughts. They are bridges and doors and entryways and foundations. They magnetize and repel. They can build a house and tear it down. They can energize momentum, or keep you idling within your own little world forever. Thoughts are investments, and they are decisions. The mind will generate an endless series of options—some inspiring, and others terrifying—and so you must choose. You must choose what you will return to, what you will believe in, what you will place weight on. Because thoughts create feeling, and feeling creates desire, and desire creates action, and action creates reward, and reward creates more desire, and before you know it, a thought became the torch that led you down the path that is your life. If you would like to change your life, you must first change the way you think about your life. There never was another way.

There is a way forward, even if you do not know what it is. You never could have predicted the precise path that led you here, and so it is not your business to control every detail. It is only your job to trust. It is only your job to focus on the next right step, and the next right step after that. Each phase brings with it a field of possibilities that our current selves could not even consider. Leave yourself open to wonder.

If you woke up tomorrow
completely healed,
who would you be?

The losses of our lives appear on the surface as abandonment and failures, but are in truth often entryways to the deepest and most powerful periods of personal growth, the moments at which we release the life we chose unconsciously, and begin to decide who we really want to be.

The truth is that you probably don't need more motivation. You already know what to do, you already know what you want, you already know what you're meant for, you already know who you are. You would choose these things without hesitation if not for the wounds, the conditioning and the limiting beliefs that prevent you from seeing clearly. You would do what you are meant to without prompt if only you knew you were allowed to, that to be your own self was not to expose yourself to more hurt, but rather, denying your truth is the most painful existence of all. The truth is that you probably don't need more motivation, you need more healing. You are not seeking a light outside of you, but to remove the blocks that are preventing you from seeing the one already radiating within.

Please, if you can, stop packing your wounds. Stop filling them up with the soil of your past, your thoughts, the things you buy and wear and drink and see. Please, if you can, stop constricting your breath, please stop folding into yourself as though you might hide the hurt so well it could disappear. I know it is the scariest thing in the world, but rinse your wounds and let them out in the light. It may hurt while it heals, but there is nothing more painful than going through the rest of your life never feeling anything new.

Everyone is here to teach you something
some through loving them
and others through losing them

If we cannot greet the day with grateful hearts, we risk all of our lives flourishing in darkness. *What if we are already sitting in a garden of miracles, and do not realize?*

Please do not confuse what is
familiar for what is right

You will soften into your soul's most honest self when you begin to see yourself with as much grace as you offer everyone else.

Everything meaningful takes time

One day, you will listen to all the songs you used to love and you will understand why you found them so beautiful.

You have already let go of so much. You have already released so many days, and all that they contained. It was never about whether or not you were able to let go, but whether or not you were willing. It was always about whether or not you would pick up tomorrow in its place.

Pain is a spellbreaking thing
it often reveals what has been
holding us back all along

You must reconcile the part of you
that feels you don't deserve so much goodness
you must slowly adapt to longer
and more heavenly states of being
you must marry your potential
you must practice your own greatness
you must weave your way out of your own doubt
you will scale the mountain
only as you master the climb

If you could only see
how many answered prayers
you have within your hands
you would never fear the future
you would never fear what's next

I know that this is hard to believe, but right now, *this is the before.* This is the beginning of the story for which no ending yet exists, because it has not been written. This is the *before.* This is what you turn back to and look upon with grateful eyes, realizing that every step set off a ripple effect that culminated into the truth of what you knew your life would become. You are not the end result of the years you spent struggling to find your way, you are just getting started.

Please don't lose another precious moment distracted by the thought of who you could have been. There are no past potentials, only what was and what became of it; only what is and what will soon be.

What's around us awakens
what's within us
the world does not happen to us
but shows us to us

I know it is hard to trust life, but it is harder not to. It is harder not to hope that there's a oneness to it all. It's harder not to believe that life itself would never create a child out of its own potential and then leave it to be lost. It is harder not to believe that everything alive exists with the intent of growth. It is harder not to believe that as you witness the various possibilities, you are being given a choice of what you want to embody. It is harder not to believe that there is a reason to it all, and on the other side, you will know exactly what it is.

The very ones with the heart to change the world are also often the ones who will fear their own destinies. They are the very ones who will be timid in the face of their own power, wondering who they might disappoint, or how they might get it wrong. They are the very ones who will fear that their contributions could never be enough. They are the very ones who will resist becoming something too unfamiliar, too strange, too different. The very ones with the drive and willingness to change the world are also often the ones with such an acute awareness of their own shortcomings, they will wonder if they deserve to be mediums for such beautiful things to occur. They are the ones who will eventually have to realize the things they thought were standing in the way of their purpose were actually the arena in which it was to take place, and that being aware of how human they are is not a shortcoming, it is a gift.

Let it light up something
sacred inside you
let it burn everything in the way

You do not see nature as perfect because it has clean lines, because it obeys everyone's desires, because it remains placid at all times. You see nature as perfect because of its wildness, its jagged edges, its unwillingness to conform to something other than what it is. You see nature as perfect because you see its power and you respect it; it simply does what it was meant to do, and does not yearn for anything more.

You are an infinite being
existing within a galaxy of infinite potential
this is not all there is

You change the world by helping others change the way they see themselves. All things are expressions of the collective, and we shift the collective one piece at a time.

You are not meant to
spend your life waiting
for your life to begin

If all is changing around you, then something is being born within you. Waves like these do not touch down upon our shorelines unless something massive has already shifted deep within.

The reason why you have been on the verge of a breakthrough for so long is because you're waiting to feel worthy enough to step foot on the other side. In the face of goodness that is so foreign and unfamiliar, you must rewrite the story that tells you how much happiness you are allowed to feel. You must go inward and decide how much life you will allow yourself to live.

Unrealistic is only
what you have not yet made real

Once the day has ended, and you are done talking about all that is wrong, once you have settled into the dim quiet, what will you have done with your own life?

Once you are finished criticizing other people and the way they look and who they've chosen to be with and what they are or are not doing, what will you have done with your own life? Once you are finished waxing poetic about all the wrongs that exist, for which there are more than most can comprehend, what will you have done with your own life?

Will you have added to the noise, or will you have brought clarity? Will you have offered your energy up to the figureheads, the supposed saviors, or will you have harnessed it for your own use? Will you have criticized others' offerings, or will you have made something of what you were given? Will you have just noticed the bad, or will you have added any good?

Was your anger an outlet for expression, or was it a tool for change? Did you make ground zero the revolution inside your own heart?

Once you have laid down in your bed, quiet, no longer arguing, no longer yearning nor hoping, and once you rise again in the morning, with swollen eyes and silence, what will you have done with your own life?

Will your thoughts have been used to construct a new world, or pick apart the ruins? Will your words have been used to lift and encourage, or suppress and push away? Will your actions have been someone's glimmer of hope, or proof that all is hopeless? Will you have done the boldest and most courageous thing, which is to look into your own unconsciousness, to see the backdrop from which you project all else? Will you have done what most could not, which is to just simply hold space for what hurts?

Though progress is slow, it exists. Evolution is the soul of all that we are.

The last moment you spent reading that sentence was experienced trillions of different ways, by trillions of different minds and bodies around the world. There is no universal experience, there is only experience and what we choose to do with it. You are not bound to what you perceive and what you think about it. The possibilities for interpretation are limitless. There will always be contrast, there will always be wisdom and wickedness.

This is what gives us the freedom to create.

Your decision must be this one resounding sentiment, one notion to drive all else, one single question: *What will I do with my own life?*

You are not a broken person
you have simply let other people
teach you how to deny yourself love
by witnessing them deny their own

What if instead of asking
what you want to do
*you began to think about
what you want to feel?*

I hope you are soft with your soul and tough with your life. I hope you can hold yourself naked at night and rise the next day to demand the world give you what you need. I hope that you can find the balance between what you must allow and what you must pursue. I hope you learn that life is a dance between what is and what will be, our highest selves and lowest impulses. I hope you will not be intimidated by all that is ahead. I hope you will know that strong minds and soft hearts often exist within the most beautiful souls.

Find stillness once again
and remember what has always been true—
you will always return to being okay
you will always return to peace

Expose yourself to the possibilities
explore all the ways life is lived
when you reach a dead end
you do not build a home there
you turn around
and see where the road goes next

The journey is about learning
that you can be completely
yourself *and be completely loved*

You did not come here
to move within a status quo
to effortlessly insert yourself
into a system unfit for you
a world unsustainable
there is only one way forward
for each of us to go inward
to dance in a way
we have never moved before

I wish someone would have told me that sometimes pain visits without purpose. Sometimes our insides ache with all of the past that we do not realize we are still holding. We will dig, and we will dig. We will hold up every fearful thought and ask, *is this what's wrong?* Even if the answer is yes, it won't matter. The feeling won't fade, and that's because it isn't supposed to. When they say listen to your gut, they mean listen to what you know, deep down, to be true. These are permeating, essential truths. These are truths we can identify with our clearest thinking and most right minds. Sometimes, when we are hurting, we prolong the experience by trying to give it meaning or cause. Sometimes, pain arrives without purpose, and if we allow it, it will leave that way, too.

You are not ordinary. There is no story like yours. There is no being like you. There is something you offer that nobody else could. Your presence on this planet has shifted it irrevocably. Without you, nothing would be the same. Please remember this when you feel small and all feels meaningless. *You are an exceptional thing.*

What if your progress so far has been the result of your willingness to dream daringly, and what if your future will unfold from the space?

You are being asked to let go
of all you've ever known
so you can receive all
you've ever asked for

There is not one person who does not need healing, because there is not one person who does not need to remember who they truly are

When you see the ones who stir envy in your heart, when you see the ones who make you doubt that you are enough, when you see the ones who make you want to withdraw from life altogether, I hope you will know that everything beautiful you see within another is what's present within yourself. I hope you will know that there is nothing you can desire that is not an inherent potential within you; *there is nothing you can desire that is something you cannot be.*

The longings that call to you are the voids asking you to fill them. You should answer. You should give yourself all you were never given, you should become all you feared you'd never be. You should fill the holes within your foundation because once they are done, you will discover life was preparing for you to build something far bigger than you could ever imagine, or truly see.

Everything exists in equilibrium. For every force there is an equal and opposite response. Our goal, then, is not to force everything into perfection, but to reside within the center, the Now, the middle-point between past and future, weaving them into a harmonious presence, allowing the highs and the lows to equally be.

No more idling
a life is to be lived

If you could only see how gorgeous
your growth has been
if you could only see how greatly
your life has changed

You exist because of centuries of love, hundreds of strangers who found one another and by some mystical, unexplainable force, chose each other—even just for a moment. Your body is the dust of the stars and the soul of your lineage. You were loved into existence. You are not here by accident, but by an astounding chance. You are a sacred thing. You will never occur in this exact way again.

You will not die once
but a thousand times
there is not just one life
within a lifetime

To see your life with new eyes
— that is the breakthrough,
and that is the path

Holy are the hands that have held you
in your hardest hours
especially when those hands
have been only your own

Your thoughts are scripting
your future into existence

Everything you've ever wanted is still waiting for you. You have not lost your chance, your potential has not waned, your truth has not diminished—even if you have kept it in hiding. All you lost was one particular chance to make it manifest. There will be an infinity more. You have not lost anything just because you lost one particular moment in time. You still contain everything you've ever wished to become.

The fog will lighten
slowly, at first
then in glimpses
in cadences of your old laughter
and your old joy
at once so familiar
and also still brand new
one day, you will remember who you are
and when you do
you will know that losing sight
only cleared your vision
it is becoming what we aren't
that shows us who we were meant to be

You get to choose how you see your life, and so I hope you choose to see serendipity. I hope that when something beautiful happens, you take it as a confirmation, and when something hard happens, you take it as a moment to rest and heal. I hope you choose to put together the pieces. I hope you seek understanding. I hope you find little wells of joy that may spring up through the day. I hope you feel a connection where others see separation. I hope you discover things you never knew you'd want to come. I hope you know that a thousand failures are the building blocks of your becoming. I hope you are not dissuaded by the dead ends; I hope you know that they are not final destinations. I hope you know that it is the courage to keep beginning that ultimately gets us all where we are meant to be.

Whatever you are afraid of confronting within the world is something you are already harboring deep within. It is not life that must be avoided, but our shadows that must be faced.

What will fill you
is what you are open to
there's an endless bounty
it pours from every corner of the earth
and from every moment in time

Effortlessness is where
the magic resides

These are the simplest facts of love.

Love is not supposed to hurt you more than it heals you. The right person makes the timing right. Indecision is a decision, and that decision is no. Love is not hard. Attachment is hard, and grief is hard, and expectations are hard. Unconscious fears are hard, and old traumas are hard. Losing a sense of security is hard. Exiting your comfort zone is hard. Facing the world alone when you thought you'd have someone to rely on is hard.

Love is not hard.

Love doesn't debate whether you should be together. Love doesn't leave you to look for signs that you should return. Love doesn't make you question whether you are worth someone's time. Love doesn't leave you doubting your interests and your quirks and the little nuances that make you who you are. Love doesn't make you feel as though you have to compete with someone else for it. Love doesn't make you prove your goodness before you can receive it.

Love is a present thing, not an abstraction. It's not something we have to wonder about or calculate. Those we love exist within our lives in real time. Love is when passion becomes presence.

You can never be perfect enough for what isn't meant to be yours. You will never be good enough for someone who has no intention of loving you.

Desire is often short-sighted
it does not see all there is
it does not know all that might be

There is not just one you that exists
you have to choose what you see
you have to choose what you become

There are only two ways to live
walking fearlessly into who we are meant to be
or watching from the sidelines
wondering when it will be our time to begin

You still have time to feel
everything you ever wanted

If you knock on a door and it remains closed, it means there is nothing behind it. There is no magical, mysterious, alternative life you are being denied. There is nothing you are missing out on. What you are grieving is an idea of what might have been. If you feel you have spent too much of your life in disappointment and regret, perhaps it is that you have tried to turn too many dead ends into pathways, empty rooms into more than they were ever intended to be. If you knock on a door and it remains closed, it means that the path is unfolding somewhere else, and you're now one step closer to finding it. It is not your dream that must be released, but your sense of possibility that must be awakened.

Pain does not arrive to punish you. It arrives to remind you that you do not deserve to be punished forever. It arrives to remind you that a different life is possible, if you have the courage to reach. It arrives to show you the space between where you are and where you are meant to be, and it lingers if you fail to bridge it. Your pain is not here to hurt you, it is here to help guide you into all you ever asked for, all you ever wanted to be.

You cannot build
your own life with the pieces
of other people's desires

If you aren't careful, your life will become defined by the four walls closest to you. You'll forget that anything else exists. Your entire world will become the perimeter of your space, and you will forget something important: past those few feet of brick and mortar exists everything. All of it. Everyone you've ever known and everyone you'll ever meet. Every story that's ever unfolded and is currently unfolding. Every shoreline, every highway, every place you've ever loved and every one you don't yet know you will. Don't let the optics trap you. You exist within an infinite universe containing infinite potentials and you, a conduit of energy and light and thought and breath and life, did not inhabit your body to just experience one tiny corner of it.

One day, you will look back on this time, and all you will see is magic. You won't remember how stuck you felt, or how far behind you thought you were, or what you wished you had done differently. All you will see is that within your uncertainty was also your potential, and within your lostness was also an opportunity to be found, and within your discomfort was also a chance to see what you needed to change, and changing it was you becoming the person you were always meant to be. If there is one single thought that can comfort you in your darkest, quietest nights, please let it be this—one day, you will look back on this time, and all you will see is magic.

I hope you allow your life to be bigger than you ever thought it could be. I hope you allow yourself to embody more beauty than you ever thought possible. I hope you don't get trapped by the small stories, the little ideas you had about what the future may be. I hope you don't long for the things you've outgrown just because they're familiar. I hope you don't consider everything you lose to be a loss. I hope you don't define yourself only by the limits of what you've known. I hope you do not cap your potential at what others have said is possible. Most of all, I hope you recognize the light when it hits you. I hope you let yourself do more than you ever thought you could.

You are going to make it, you know
you are going to become
all that you've ever wanted to be

If you look with your eyes, all you will see are relics of the past. You must have vision. You must be willing to imagine what does not yet exist, and then be willing to believe that it one day might.

The past and future are dreams within the Now, easily disrupted by the mind's endless interpretation of what might be. Don't let it run too far ahead or behind. The Now is the only place of true peace.

Anything you desire is possible
everything you envision can be

Healing is not something you do once. It is a way you learn to bring yourself back from every disappointment and defeat. It is how you learn to soothe yourself, to validate the way you feel. It is how you learn to take care of yourself, and to bring you back to the person you are meant to be. Healing is not something you do once and then never again, it is a way of living that allows you to no longer carry what hurts, it's a way of living that allows you to walk free.

If you cannot let go of what has passed
anchor your energy into the future
imagine how you will walk through life
in just a few years time
instead of being held by what haunts you
be pulled by what calls you
gravitate toward your biggest truth
even if all the smaller minded ones
coexist beside it

Don't go forward.

First, go inward.

Right here.

Spend nights in candlelight with a journal. Take days of opening your mind to possibilities you didn't know existed. Study the contours of your body, exactly as it is. Decorate yourself in what you want to be. Dance naked. Come home to yourself. Apologize. Hold space for your old selves as they are leaving you now. Say thank you to everything that has gotten you this far.

The only way forward is inward, and the only way out is through.

When you spend time acquainting yourself with your soul, something magical occurs—you wake up one day and the world is different. The answers come. The next right step is revealed to you, and then the next right one after that. You're led to where you were always meant to be—not farther from where you started, but back to who you've been the entire time.

Even though we aren't always
given what we wanted
we are somehow always
handed what we need

If you are more concerned
with being misunderstood
than misunderstanding
with how your life is seen
instead of how it is felt
in maintaining who you aren't
instead of becoming who you are
then you really haven't started to live at all yet
have you?

There is someone out there who will hold all of you. There is someone out there who will make love feel like the easiest thing in the world. There is someone out there who will accept every part of you. There is someone out there who will make you feel like the most obvious choice. There is someone out there with whom you will build a life, and with whom a lifetime won't feel like enough.

There is nothing in the universe
that can keep you from who you really are
and what you are really meant to do
you may harden your heart to it
but it will always be there
waiting for you to awaken again

You came to do what can only be done right here, right now, just like this. You are only here for a moment. You only exist for a breath. I hope you savor every second. *I hope you do not waste any more time.*

The story is already written
time is just a trick of the mind

You are already there
you have already arrived

You are just remembering
what's always been

Nobody really learns how to let go, you just learn how to allow something else to capture your soul. You learn how to make something else matter more. You learn how to immerse yourself in the life you are building instead of the one you have left. Nobody really learns how to let go, you just learn how to build something new in the place of what was supposed to be.

It is not what we aren't capable
of that holds us back, but the fear
that we don't deserve the life our
most capable selves could create

You deserve beautiful things to happen to you. You deserve miracles. You deserve to be loved in every way you ever dreamed you could be. You deserve everything you have worked and waited for. *You deserve a good life.* You deserve good things to happen to you. You deserve to feel everything you ever wanted, and you deserve to know that life is one infinite possibility.

Beneath all of your other longings
is a steady current
a place you will always return to
no matter how far you stray
one that bridges where you are
and what you're meant to be
within that constant
is every answer
which is really just one answer
what you came to do—
which is become yourself

You were never meant
to find permanent peace
in a temporary world
but rather at a place deep within you
where love always lives

You don't need to wash away every doubt before you can start walking toward all you are meant to be.

Don't worry about taking apart
what you no longer desire
focus only on the vision of what will replace it
and let the rest fall into the fire of time

Let it all come apart at its own pace
and in its own way

You need not know how every leaf
will fall from the trees
you only need to trust that winter will come
and the earth will once again be reborn

When you can look into the eyes of a stranger and see your own soul, then you will know you are really alive.

You are here to
alchemize reality
you are here to heal your
piece of the whole

You did not come as far as you have, through as much as you did, across all of the unknown you've faced, for it to end here. You did not embark on this journey to return to passivity, to become the most mild and acceptable version of yourself. You began in order to live boldly, to embrace yourself as a field of contradictions, to release yourself into the moment and let it take you where it may. You did not go through everything you have just to stop now, just to become something familiar to someone else's eyes, but foreign to your own heart. You walked this path to get to the other side, please don't stop when you finally see the horizon.

You are an electric stream of light
an embodiment of an ancient universe
completely your own and yet
one in the same
with everyone and everything

How could you ever think
that you exist without purpose?
how could you ever think
you are a meaningless occurrence?
how could you ever assume
you only came here to hurt
but never to see the other side?

Leave nothing unturned
nothing unseen
nothing saved for a someday
that might never come

You cannot heal your way to a world where negativity doesn't exist, because it always will. You cannot heal your way into the most physically perfect version of yourself, because that's not who you were born and built to be. You cannot heal your way out of every worry, issue, struggle, grief, sadness, or down day, because that's not the point of being alive. The point of healing is not to return to a place where everything is perfect, it is to develop the ability to respond to what's imperfect. You cannot heal your way out of being human, and you were never supposed to.

The world is waiting to receive what you are longing to give. Please do not think living out your purpose is somehow a burden upon the world. It is a beacon of what is possible. It is a testament to the truth that resides within us all. Please walk without fear, for you are forging a new path, making a new way of existing—a way for other souls to follow.

This is for the disruptors
the change-makers
the karma-breakers
the pivot characters

This is for the ones who will live differently
so that generations to follow
will experience life differently

This is for the ones who follow a path
with no blueprint
an existence with no precedence

You are unlike this world
because your purpose is not
to adapt well to a world that is unwell
but to carve out your own universe
within this one

If you have been given the gift of vision
beyond what most eyes can see
may you be courageous enough
to make it manifest
and may it change everything
for us all

Let yourself evolve

You have lost nothing
but what could not sustain itself any longer
you have lost nothing but what was ending anyway
you have lost nothing but an idea of what the future
might have been

All that is real is still waiting
all that is real is still within

We are recycled stardust

we contain everything possible

Do not let anyone convince you
that you cannot build something beautiful
out of what's been broken

If you ever get the chance, go alone
walk alone, travel alone, live alone, dance alone
just for a night, just for a while

If you ever get the chance
learn who you are when the world isn't demanding
you be one way or another

Most people only know how to stand
if someone else is beside them
don't let that be your story

If you ever get the chance
know that the opportunity to walk alone
even for a short while
is a gift unlike any other
one that can hand you insight
that can change the rest of your life

Stop asking for permission
for what is already yours

Is knowing that joy cannot last forever a reason to not let yourself feel it at all?

Your life will pass one way or another. The events that will unfold are the events that will unfold, you will meet who you are meant to, you will find the opportunities you need. The choice is not what you experience, but how. How is everything. How is golden. How closes doors and it opens them. How creates something out of nothing. It is not the years we live, but how we live them. It is not who we cross paths with, but how we love them. It is not what we are given or not, but how we take what's in front of us and turn it into all we ever needed it to be. It is how we experience life—day in, and day out, in the quietest moments and biggest ways. The how is the way.

Our power isn't found
in what exists
but in how we respond
to what exists

The water does not climb over mountains
it finds the easiest path
and flows
one of nature's most shaping weapons
is the subtle flow of water
that can corrode and carve and change
and the same is true
of whatever flows through our souls

If you are looking for a sign, looking for something to convince you that you are enough for your own destiny—you will have to start with the first emboldening thing, which is to feel your life from the inside instead of perceiving it from the outside.

You can no longer look for love from an invisible audience. You will have to decide that living in accordance with your innermost truth is your top priority, for which anything can be risked and everything must. You will have to decide the extent to which you are willing to meet your soul at the mountaintop, how far you will climb and how much you will care and how deeply you will commit to the work, because *this is work.*

You will have to say goodbye to certainties. The things that make people feel less fear, but not more alive. You will have to draft a vision for what you could see your life becoming. You will need to be ambitious, because if you're going to go for it, you need to go all the way.

You will have to start where you are. You will have to be humbled. You will have to stop knocking at the door, and build your own hallway. You will have to test and try and change things. You will have to reinvent your self-image.

You will have to stop asking for permission. You will have to stop thinking one person's perspective of you is the sum of who you are. You will have to show up—again, and again, and again. You will have to create—again, and again, and again.

Then you will have to see what arrives, and what remains. Watch for what works. Wait for what is effortless. All of the pieces will come together. You just have to be willing to start.

There is a path
to everything you've ever wanted
there is a way
to everything you've ever seen

Even at your most broken, the right person will look at you like you are the most beautiful thing in the world. Wait for the one who sees you as all you could be and all you already are. Wait for the one who chooses you no matter how inconvenient it is, no matter how little sense it makes, no matter what they must disrupt within their lives to ensure it will merge with yours. Wait for the one who sees you as you really are. Wait for the one who makes all the waiting worth it.

I hope you find the courage to change your life. In the small ways, in the big ways, in every way that matters. I hope you do not end this story with a heart full of regrets. I hope you do not spend your years just waiting for your life to begin. I hope you realize that this is not the practice run, this is not the preview. This is it. There is nothing to do but leap. There is nothing to do but allow yourself to exist as boldly and honestly as you can. You will think you have forever, but you do not. It all happens, and it happens quickly. You are not waiting on another person, or the right timing, or for everything to fall into place. You are waiting to feel ready enough to exist within the questions, to not need every answer, and to know that this life does not come to us to be perfectly understood, but to be fully experienced, in every direction we can possibly reach.

BRIANNA WIEST is a writer based in Phila-delphia. She aims to share words that encourage awareness and self-understanding. Brianna is the author of seven books, including the bestselling essay collection *101 Essays That Will Change The Way You Think*. Brianna's work has been seen in publications such as *The Huffington Post, USA Today, Medium, Forbes*, and more. She is currently a partner at Thought Catalog.

BRIANNAWIEST.COM

INSTAGRAM.COM/BRIANNAWIEST

TWITTER.COM/BRIANNAWIEST

MORE FROM BRIANNA WIEST

101 Essays That Will Change The Way You Think

The Mountain Is You

Salt Water

I Am The Hero Of My Own Life

The Truth About Everything

THOUGHT CATALOG Books

THOUGHTCATALOG.COM
NEW YORK · LOS ANGELES